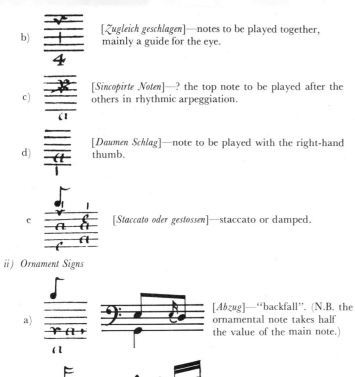

b) [*Zugleich geschlagen*]—notes to be played together, mainly a guide for the eye.

c) [*Sincopirte Noten*]—? the top note to be played after the others in rhythmic arpeggiation.

d) [*Daumen Schlag*]—note to be played with the right-hand thumb.

e) [*Staccato oder gestossen*]—staccato or damped.

ii) Ornament Signs

a) [*Abzug*]—"backfall". (N.B. the ornamental note takes half the value of the main note.)

b) [*Einfall*]—"forefall".

c) Trill. (N.B. from the upper note—this ornament is merely an extended form of a.)

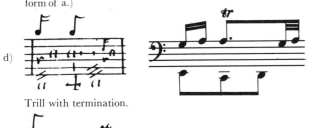

d) Trill with termination.

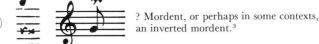

e) ? Mordent, or perhaps in some contexts, an inverted mordent.[3]

f) (normally notated) [*Bebung*]—vibrato.

g) (? = Beyer's *Circulo mezzo*) a turn?

Circulo mezzo.

Straube's efforts to render his tablature as explicit as possible (like keyboard notation) result in some unusual forms of notation. Two of these are ties and what might be called "grace letters". For example, ties are occasionally notated thus:

"Grace letters" (i.e. small letters with their own small rhythm signs immediately above them) are rarely inserted in *Sonata I*, but in *Sonata II* they are frequent. Their commonest use is for indicating the termination of a trill (see above). Sometimes they simply make clear the correct auxiliary note for playing an ornament already notated by sign, e.g.:

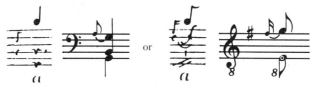

or

But there are also cases where the note could not be easily notated by a sign, e.g.:

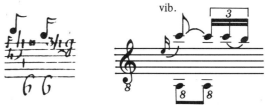

vib.

or when the length of the ornament would not be clear from a sign, e.g.:

These "grace letters" should be played *on* the beat, as their counterparts in the conventional keyboard notation of the time would have been, rather than *before* the beat, as their position on the stave might suggest.

Tim Crawford
London, January 1981

FOOTNOTES

[1] Copied from *The Four Ages of Man; together with Essays on Various Subjects*, London 1798, by William Jackson of Exeter, p. 151f, part of an essay on Gainsborough:

"...upon seeing a Theorbo in a picture of Vandyke's; he concluded (perhaps, because it was finely painted) that the Theorbo must be a fine instrument. He recollected to have heard of a German professor, who, though no more, I shall forbear to name ... ascended *per varios gradus* to his garret, where he found him at dinner upon a roasted apple, and smoking a pipe...."

Straube's name has been supplied throughout in the Add 31698 MS extract. The lute which Gainsborough bought from Straube (apparently for ten guineas) became part of his large and valuable collection of famous musicians' instruments, and seems to have been sold together with a Spanish Guitar for £2 10s to John Hoppner R.A., the famous portraitist, by Gainsborough's daughter Margaret in 1799.

[2] The German names in brackets come from Johann Christian Beyer's *Herrn Professor Gellerts Oden, Lieder und Fabeln, ... für die Laute übersetzt*, Leipzig 1760, which contains a useful table, although some signs are used differently.

[3] In Adam Falckenhagen's *Sonate*, Nuremburg c. 1740, the two types of mordent are distinguished—the sign used by Straube meaning an inverted mordent, but with another sign ( ) for a normal mordent. (The latter sign is so interpreted in an ornament table in Nuremburg Germanisches Museum MS 274, a manuscript associated with Bayreuth during Falckenhagen's employment there.)

Due Sonate
a Liuto Solo
Composte
da Rudolfo Straube
Academico in Lipsia

dedicate

A SUA ECCELLENZA

Il Signore CARLO HENRICO di DIESKAV

Signore di Knauthain, Kleinzschocher e Cospuden &c.

Camerlengo di S. M. il Rè di Pologna ed Elettor di Sassonia

e Capitano del Circolo di Lipsia. &c.

In Verlegung des Autoris.

Lipsia l'anno
1746
intagl: da Schönemann

ILLUSTRISSIMO SIGNORE

All'ECCELLENZA VOSTRA com'egregio amatore, quanto compitissimo Conoscitore, della Musica anzi del Liuto vengono umilissimamente dedicate le premizie della mia diligenza impiegata a questo stromento, ed avendo io parechie volte potuto accorgermi distintamente da un pezzo in quà dell'alto SUO Favore verso di me spero che V.E. si compiacerà, d'interpretar in buona parte l'ardidezza mia, di giudicar favorevolmente di quest'Opera, e di degnarmi dell'ulteriore grazia SUA il che mi spronerà d'applicarmi all'avvenire anche con maggior caldezza alla musica Io intanto pregarò Iddio che colmi l'ECCELLENTISSIMA SUA persona com'anche l'ILL.ma casa SUA con ogni vera ed immutabil prosperità essendo con ogni maggior umiltà senza mai finire

di VOSTRA ECCELLENZA

umill.mo e divotiss.mo
Servitore
Rudolfo Straube.

4

Sonata II